Etymology of Courage

Also by Gabrielle Journey Jones and published by
Ginninderra Press
Spoken Medicine

Gabrielle Journey Jones

Etymology of Courage

Acknowledgements

Some poems appear on Gabrielle's Poetic Percussion website as videos and in print at www.poeticpercussion.com.au
'Spoken Words' was published in *Wild*, Ginninderra Press 2018
'Wait Till You See Thirroul' in *Mountain Secrets*, Ginninderra Press 2019 (in shorter form)'
'Women are Reclaiming our Lives in *I Protest: Poems of Dissent*, Ginninderra Press 2020 (in shorter form)
'Unspoken Things' in *Women of the Word*, Papatuanuku Press
'Girl Guidelines' in *Alphabet of Women* by Poetica
'Preach Poets' in *Unspoken Words Festival 2018* chapbook by Unspoken Words Collective
'First Impressions' in *Dreaming Inside*, vol. 6, 2018
'Desert Sand' was written and performed for Saba Vasefi Films, 2020
'Release' and 'Here Now' are edited poetry samples from *Tripple Treat* project with Lisa and Steve Hughes, 2018
'Silence We Carry' written by Gabrielle Journey Jones after consultation with *Circus WOW (Women of Wollongong) Adagio*, directed by Jane Davis

Etymology of Courage
ISBN 978 1 76109 099 8
Copyright © text Gabrielle Journey Jones 2021
Cover art: Amalina Wallace

First published 2021 by
GINNINDERRA PRESS
PO Box 3461 Port Adelaide 5015
www.ginninderrapress.com.au

Dedication

This anthology is dedicated to everyone brave enough to share their truth and stories creatively through spoken word poetry. Massive love and appreciation to all the wordsmiths that I am lucky enough to call my friends, and to family, who 'stand in front of others courageously, feverish with poetry' ('Spoken Words', page 11).

courage (n.) c. 1300, corage, 'heart (as the seat of emotions)', hence 'spirit, temperament, state or frame of mind', from Old French corage 'heart, innermost feelings; temper' (12c., Modern French courage), from Latin cor 'heart'.
Source: https://www.etymonline.com/word/courage

Gratitude

I have the greatest blessing of raising Jai and Sofara, my two courageous hearts who share my passion for creativity. I thank them for their unconditional love and joy. They had wonderful grandfathers, Poppy Jones (Bega) and Poppy Trevor (Thirroul), who both passed away in 2019. I am grateful for the three generations of family that surrounded me – our individual journeys and collective strengths – as I penned and performed the poems in this collection.

Open-hearted thanks to my mother Patricia Jones for proofreading and lifelong moral support; Amalina Wallace for her delightful cover art and long-term contribution to the energy of this project; and Brenda Matthews for professional support and editing.

Thanks also to Merrily Black for my author photo and the other artists who have shared work which has inspired poetry in this collection – Wendy Gibson, Tanja Ponsford, Christine Linn Quinton and Circus WOW.

Much appreciation to Ginninderra Press for the opportunity to be part of their diverse, inspiring poetry community. This collection was collated and edited on Djiringanj Land, Yuin Country, Far South Coast of NSW, Australia. Always was and always will be Aboriginal land.

Contents

Heart Craft
- Spoken Words — 11
- Preach, Poets! — 12
- Unspoken Things — 14
- Outrageous! — 15
- Degustation — 16
- Manuscript Offering — 17

Heart Womyn
- Women Are Reclaiming Our Lives — 21
- Healing Our Stories — 23
- Silence We Carry — 25
- Girl Guidelines — 28
- Disclosure Renaissance — 29
- Set Them Free — 30
- What's Her Story? — 31

Heart Places
- Wait Till You See Thirroul — 35
- Austinmer Summer — 37
- Coledale Sunrise — 38
- What Brings Us To Bega? — 39
- Bigga River Walks — 42
- Haberdashery Hills of Bemboka — 43
- Bemboka Trio — 44
- Bundjalung Pinball Dawn — 45
- Leaving Desert Womb — 46
- Burning Seed Belonging — 47
- Redbelly Farm Reminders — 48

Heart Lessons

Desert Sand Remembers	51
Trauma Stories	52
Exit Wounds	53
Haunted	54
Life Hacks	55
Wondering	56
First Impressions	57
Ekphrasis Inferno	59
Last Harvest	61
Remembrance	63

Heart Solace

Kia Kaha Stay Strong	69
Finally Fine	73
Settle	74
Release	76
Here Now	77
Joy Philosophy	78

Heart Craft

Spoken Words

Feverish with poetry
Spitting tortured rhymes
Into the faded mesh of a microphone
Hoping to flush wild words away.

On the out-breath
Of unspoken voices
Amplified chaos
Traces of our stories
Become more bearable
Soothing the sensation
That we are barely here at all.

Even if we only show up
Inside a lonely moment on stage
Oscillating between heartbreak
And justifiable rage!

Even if we only expel
Truncated versions of our pain
When we speak about others
We speak of our own resilience.

We replay and reframe
Narratives that would claim us
Captives of silence and shame.
Voluntarily we stand in front
Of others courageously
Feverish with poetry.

Preach, Poets!

Poetry is the soapbox I stand on
Express my demands from
Advocate resistance
To oppressive systems
In rhyme form.

I won't massage metaphors
To make my words digestible.
I don't use too many similes
To beautify my views, you see
When we speak our truth clearly
We invoke visibility.

What once was hidden
Unheard and unseen
Becomes vital points of difference
Not just secrets unspoken
Labelled 'less than'
Considered broken
Leaving us feeling unwelcome
Watching our words and stories
Overwhelm them
Some even try to sanitise
and retell them.

Let's break in!
Let's steal token notions
Of 'Acceptable poems'
Let's refuse silence
Let's review self-censorship
Reject creative compliance
Let's keep our integrity in alignment.

If there are no safe spaces
For our truth to be outspoken
Let's join together our soapboxes
So others can find us
And let's preach, poets!
Preach!

Unspoken Things

There are unspoken things
Mostly silenced fears
Sometimes truth
That we are afraid of being perceived:
Anxious, overwhelmed, overprotective.
We dare not admit any of this to ourselves.
Therefore, these things can never be written
They can never be rehearsed or spoken
They remain consciously unknown.

There are unspoken things
Mostly heart sorrows
Sometimes truth
That we have endless words
In the shape of poems about.
Stashed in dark corners of our house
They surprise us when we forgetfully
Unearth them during annual clean outs.
But we cannot bring ourselves to read them
At least never, ever aloud.

There are unspoken things
Mostly personal trauma
Sometimes truth
That we doubt others can bear our telling.
We are continually unsure about permissions
In this society sick and swelling
Bloated with the stench of secrets
We are expected to leave unspoken.

Outrageous!

How dare your poems make marks on this paper!
These pages have slain the bravest narrators
You claim you're courageous? Don't care about haters?
You just want your truth liberated? Outrageous!

How dare your spontaneous
Symphony of words brash and deafening
Spring from your pen like the wisdom of sages!
Who gives you permission to say what needs saying?

You act like it's a birthright to display what you're feeling
You tune into yourself then hold a public revealing
Revelling in the romance of spoken word performance
You hope to connect with a click of recognition?

The human condition is a shared experience?
Creative expression helps you breathe into the present?
A lifetime of waiting for collective reflection
Witnessed on supportive open mic stages? Outrageous!

Degustation

She dines on poetry.
She slurps random letters slowly
Enjoying the chaos of alphabet soup
Jumbled about in her mouth
Leaving a minestrone tang on her tongue.

She dines on poetry.
She crunches crispy spring rolls
Front teeth first as filo pastry falls
Onto her chin like an initial edit
Of superfluous words.

She dines on poetry.
She carves into a steaming slice of lasagne
Aubergine aroma rhythmically
Rising through béchamel sauce
Sautéed vegetables tell assorted stories
She collects in chapters on her fork and devours.

She dines on poetry.
She navigates scoops of Neapolitan ice cream
Lavishly typeset on coconut chia pudding
Coaxing chocolate and strawberry onto her spoon
Finally satiated by her delicious selection of verse.

Manuscript Offering

Ring bound
Running rings around
The last profound offering.
Words folded inside manila folders
Like worlds falling down
Finally, boundless
Floating groundless
A pound of flesh
Would be less stress
Than all of these chapters mounted
Like a sermon on a mountain
Delivered unto the public gaze
Sanctified inside the pages of this manuscript
Fictitious scriptures flipped as present-day parables
Subliminal metaphors and secrets turned similes
Ring bound
Running rings around
The last profound offering.

Heart Womyn

Women Are Reclaiming Our Lives

Women are reclaiming our nights
Stolen by perpetrators of sexual violence
Robbed by emotional abuse and threats of poverty
We imagine not having to fight for our lives
Not having to train our bodies, hearts and minds
In daily self-defence and constant vigilance
We should be safe in every space we occupy
After dark and in broad daylight.

Women are reclaiming our rights
To physical and financial freedom
We imagine a world created for our wellbeing
Where going home is to the safest
Sanctuary we have ever known
Where legal systems protect victims
And 'No' is respected as 'No'
Where women's bodies remain unharmed
'Whatever we wear, wherever we go.'

Women are reclaiming our choices
We celebrate our strength and resilience
We imagine words we finally breathe unafraid
Shattering the power of domestic silence
Every time that we speak our truth without shame
Every attempt that we make to regain our options
No longer chained by gendered domination.

Women are reclaiming our voices
We march with megaphones on main streets
Chanting women's rights to drum beats
Reclaim the Night began in Leeds back in '77
Women of the world still hold the vision
We gather globally to protest and advocate
All the ways that our lives are being reclaimed
From all forms of violence, rape and hate.

Healing Our Stories

Mothers are speaking loud!
Casting our secrets out
We're healing our stories

Our truth transforms trauma
Transcends trigger warnings
We're healing our stories

Through gendered displacement
We're claiming our spaces
We're healing our stories

We're mothers creative
We're fearless, we got this
We're healing our stories

We're teaching our children
To tune in and listen
We're healing our stories

We march against violence
Refuse to be silent
We're healing our stories

Despite lies and abuse
We're living how we choose
We're healing our stories

We're victors not victims
Disrupting the system
We're healing our stories

Sisterhood resilience
We rise, we shine brilliant
We're healing our stories

Mothers are speaking loud!
Casting our secrets out
We're healing our stories

Silence We Carry

Written for Circus WOW Adagio

I am a woman who is expected to be nurturing
I am a woman who is expected to survive everything
I am a woman who is expected to be strong
I am a woman who is expected to comply with silence
This is the silence I carry, this is the silence we carry

I am a woman who is expected to be nurturing
Irrespective of a world that does not nurture me
A world that demands I should accept such betrayal of trust
Found in the hypothesis thrust upon women by systems of injustice
That sexual violence against us is not only inevitable, but untouchable

I am a woman who is expected to survive everything
I am expected to keep others protected
From the septic effects of secondary trauma poisoning
All of my hidden stories come with trigger warnings
And I am supposed to survive everything
Without sharing or complaining
It is easier not to mention anything
I am supposed to pretend the parts of my body
Brutally stolen from me in a million acts of aggression
Is my own fault or my imagination!

I am a woman who is expected to survive everything
Alone. Independently. Invisibly held, cradled
Supported by women before me
Escaping violent herstories
Inherently present on a women's journey
This is the silence I carry, this is the silence we carry

I am a woman who is expected to be strong
I carry invisible stories of silence and shame
I carry invisible stories of anger and anxiety
I carry invisible stories of self-doubt and powerlessness
My invisible stories are undetected detonators
Of vulnerability truth bombs
In frozen fearful moments when terror wins
Defeated I decide on fundamental things:

Not to let my beauty shine through my smile
Not to wear whatever I want at anytime
Not to walk solo under moonlit sky
Not to attend evening events alone
Not to feel safe outside my home

I am a woman who is expected to be strong
But I carry some of my invisible stories
Hidden in plain sight hoping to leave signs
In the way I hold my car keys at night
Gripped tight, metal part upright
Fists in a ball prepared for flight!

I am a woman who is expected to comply with silence
Not just comply with it, but be complicit in it
Intentionally apply silence until my sisters agree with it
Hold no space or time to ever bear witness
To shocking stories of sexual abuse
It's another method that we all use
To flee the reality of it

It's true, sometimes I hide from the impact of it
Inside the comfort of silence and lies
So I don't have to believe any of it and I don't have to relive any of it
So WE don't have to believe any of it and WE don't have to relive any of it
This is the silence I carry, this is the silence we carry

I am a woman who is expected to be nurturing
I am a woman who is expected to survive everything
I am a woman who is expected to be strong
I am a woman who is expected to comply with silence
I am a woman who continues to survive

Girl Guidelines

Grind gutsy goals
Graciously
Guard against garrulous
Gossipers
Gather goofy sniggering
Giggles
Grasp digestible gratitude
Graphically
Guzzle gullible guilt
Gallantly
Galvanize guaranteed goodness
Generously
Grieve intergenerational
Gentrification
Glimpse glimmering forgotten
Galaxies.

Disclosure Renaissance

Writing this decade
Into existence
Instagram truth
Integrated flash fiction
Keyboard warriors
Advocacy of insistence
Powered by perseverance
Disclosure Renaissance
Rebellion, resistance!

Womoon writers
Visionaries believing
Solutions we scribe
Motivates activism
Global sanctions
Demanding repair
Of sinister damaging
Dangerous negligence!

Divulging deceptions
Intersectional feminisms
Collectively our voices
Distinguish us from victims.

Set Them Free

Women my age need the Fashion Police to know
That brassieres are wickedly uncomfortable
We only wear them so everyone else
Can feel comfortable and stop judging us.

But as soon as we get home we unhook and discard
These modern-day corsets, we fling them on the floor
The minute we cross our front doorstep!
Unchain our body from ten hours
Inside expensive elastic and painful wire bars
That hold us captive like two criminals arrested
If we dare to enter society with our breasts unfettered.

Imagine women moving around unashamed
Our whole being harmoniously unrestricted?
Women are taught that this is not acceptable
It's barely tolerable to feed our babies in public.

Bras are ergonomically functional
But what function do they really perform?
When women cannot wait to be set free
To finally be liberated and restored
At the end of every single day
In privacy behind our closed doors.

What's Her Story?

Inspired by the Art of Christine Linn Quinton

What's her story?
She is creating art!
She is art!
She is self-expression!
She is daring to be seen!

Sculpting life, painting visions
Honouring her memories
Sharing her imagination.
Here. Now.

A collage in a box
Her ideas and images
Protected behind a colourful
Criss-cross of knitting wool
Yellow, pink, green and indigo.

A heart hanging in a box
Pulsating for a safer earth
So that her grandchildren
Will have a planet to inherit.

An angel on a box
Her clay wings unfurled
Wishing International Women's Day
Blessings upon the world.

What's her story?
She is creating art!
She is art!
She is self-expression!
She is daring to be seen!

Heart Places

Wait Till You See Thirroul

Wait till you see
The way the escarpment behind us
Curves around and kisses the ocean beside us.
Just like new lovers excited to see each other
Staring in disbelief that they have finally found each other!
They will cling to each other for another 40 million years
Besotted by the untameable, effortless splendour between them
Sparks of magic and joy hanging above their heads
At night as dancing stars and by day as the sweltering summer sun.

Wait till you see
How the green of these gum trees and the gold of this seashore
Really are fair dinkum mates to anyone in times of need.
In need of shade to stop and rest
In need of water to feel weightless
In need of safe ears to whisper unsafe secrets
To be spirited away with the ebb tide.

Wait till you wake in the morning
And hear the sweetest birdsong creating a valley of harmonies
So gently ricocheting through the belly of this mountain range
That their music will drift you back to sleep.

Wait till you see the spectacular formation of stratus clouds
Ascending a sunrise journey along our lush green foothills
Hovering over narrow bush tracks as if checking for injured wildlife
Before allowing a new day to birth beneath its softening mist.

Wait till you see
The translucent yellow glow of dawn
Electrify our metallic blue ocean horizon
Like a desert mirage shimmering its way towards
The outstretched crescent arms of Thirroul Beach.
Local surfers at day break form a moving mandala
A joyous meditation on the simple gifts
Of Mother Nature: golden sunlight on salt water
Framed by Mount Bulli, Dharawal Land.

Wait till you wade in waist deep
And truly meet with this part of the Pacific Ocean
She is constantly moving but she soothes me still
She is grounding. She anchors life with her depth
She dances enchanted by incantations of moon
Rising and falling, rising and falling, rising and falling
And returning to herself; yet calling me home.
She leaves the most delightful patterns
In the darkest sand at the turn of her tides
Like coded love letters to the sentinel escarpment
Willingly and forever by her side.
I can't wait till you see Thirroul.

Austinmer Summer

Summer's returning
On the bubbling foam
Of these breaking waves

Summer's returning
On the bait on the hook
for this fisherman's prey

Summer's returning
On the bench at the beach
In those lovers' soft gaze

Summer's returning
On the cracks in the ozone
Sending through sunburnt rays

Summer's returning
On the face of the surf club clock
On these lengthening days.

Coledale Sunrise

Ocean waves purple, indigo
Quarter moon in this pale blue
Sky, rising sun burning white
Too bright to look directly.

Mountain side, quiet road
Slide eyes down grassy slope
Tents and caravans elope
Only savvy surfers surface
Worshipping Winter's horizon.

Wind dances under my camper
Inviting my feet out into the sand.
I return to sleep snuggled in doonas.
Solitary seaside mornings are rare.

What Brings Us To Bega?

We are the lucky ones
Tree-change adventures
Treasures of the ocean nearby
Every week or so
Someone asks me why:
'What brings you to Bega?'

We value this village atmosphere
Living in our own regional
Australian TV show
Sharing the unpretentious
Charm of Wandin Valley
We have discovered
A country practice of kindness.

Everyone has been welcoming
Everyone here is polite
Generous with genuine smiles
Solid handshakes
Enthusiastic advice
Everyone here is nice.

I've heard brave stories
Hardships of the land
Heartaches of the soul
Or both, too often both
Survivors all, and they will
Walk an extra kilometre
For strangers as much as friends
Never bothered by the distance.

I don't hesitate to answer
This persistent question:
'What brings you to Bega?'

Our peaceful country abode
From a deckchair on our veranda
Mumbulla mountain is an oil painting
Changeable moods waiting for us
Each morning when we pause
Outside to appreciate the view.

A collection of small hills surround us
Comforting and constant
Like my childhood landscape
Growing up in Canberra
On Ngunnawal Country.

Bega is Djiringanj Land
Umbarra Black Duck totem
White cockatoos patrol in their dozens
I can see dairy cows grazing
While I'm hanging out the washing
There's a bike path to the river
Right across the road inviting us
To skim stones and swim.

Our street lights are so far apart
The Milky Way fills the darkness
Close enough to stir those stars
With our fingertips and trace
Constellations above our house.

The place I have always felt safest
Is my parents' home.
When my father became unwell
My children and I moved to Bega
To be here for his final journey.

Underneath this enchanting Yuin sky
Held within this friendly community
Connected to our loving family
All of this, is what keeps us in Bega.

A Country Practice was an Australian TV show 1981–1994 set in a fictitious town, Wandin Valley, NSW.

Bigga River Walks

Bigga River is a temple of quietude
We walk our demons and angels
Around the abandoned racecourse

Along the gravel pathway we speak secrets
Into drought-weary casuarina trunks
We stop to touch textures in the bark

We send our intimate stories
Through leafy winter canopies
Wishes assigned to the universe.

Haberdashery Hills of Bemboka

Inspired by the art of Wendy Gibson

Sewing ripe green farmland
To this daydream azure sky
With wild, dark stitches
Of serrated mountain.
A patchwork of cloud
Carrying the echo of rain
Could be a blessing or curse
During these uncertain times
Depending on Mother Earth's
Most recent memories.

Bemboka Trio

Inspired by the photography of Wendy Gibson

Three trees on separate banks
Reach across a glassy creek
Shadows interconnected
Reflections mirrored.

Nature holds nature
In its own gentle gaze
Fuschia flames of dawn
Form butterfly wings
Where clouds and water join
Pinned on outstretched branches.

A millisecond of morning
Meanders through her lens
Blinked into this moment
By atmospheric pleasure
In resounding pastel colours.

Bundjalung Pinball Dawn

Cars slide along the foothills
Like marbles in a pinball machine
Silent from this distance
Underneath a satin pillowslip of fog.

Shooting across the asphalt horizon from both directions
Right button rolls them in from the Pacific Ocean
Left pushes them out from the sleeping city of Lismore
Into town, out of town, headlights still on
Night shift swaps with the early morning workers.

Witnessed from behind the rectangular frame
Of this kitchen window which doubles
As the top of an arcade game
Painted at the base in every shade of green
For the trees and the low-lying mountains.

Clusters of ghost gums, jacarandas and eucalypts
A zigzag of streets criss-cross towards the glass
Red-tiled roofs reflecting the sunrise
Charolais cows grazing on breakfast grass.

The sides are light blue, dusted with clouds
And on the far wall of this unique
Mesmerising pinball dawn landscape
Float two exquisite hot air balloons
In red and gold, rising into the winter sky.

Leaving Desert Womb

I took the deepest breath
Exhaled, a little scared but mostly proud
As I drove through my cocoon
The wise old Arrernte caterpillar gap
knowing that this afternoon sun
will dry my sparkling new butterfly wings
Allowing me to fly freely now
Almost unfurled braving the world
Decorated in turquoise for wisdom
with golden edgings of bright yellow.

Burning Seed Belonging

Humanity embodied effigies
A trio of timber-crafted
Guardians stand statuesque
Three metres high and wide
Balancing a wooden globe
Across their broad shoulders
Waiting for the flame.

Three thousand witnesses
Intentional community
Revelry on the Paddock
Flamboyant costumes
Deep trance music
Laughter and happiness
Drummers signal the ritual
Fire sticks dance brightly
Symbolism alight
Burning the Man!

Emblazoned radical self-expression
Artistry, participation, self-reliance
Decommodification of oppression
Shared wonderment and reflection
Enveloped in our conscious belonging.

My children and I watched mesmerised
Wind whipped dusty spirals of fire
Three million discarded hot embers
Dissolved into Wiradjuri midnight.

Redbelly Farm Reminders

Too often cities forget they are incomplete
Too depleted, too deep in concrete
Too crowded, loud and indiscreet.

No farmland backyards with roosters and hens
No wet grass for bare feet to enjoy after rain
No clean air, no rugged bush walking terrain.
No ocean moonrise on the horizon.

No secret starlit lakes down the hill
No melancholy long-distant views
No way to measure happiness
By hours spent without shoes.

No mist on summer's breeze at 8pm
No warm country welcome
No spontaneous pesto pasta
No storm-gazing with new friends.

No horse at the window
No dogs in the beds
No birdsong, no frog songs
No mountains to depend on.

No further reminders needed.
No more cities for me.

Heart Lessons

Desert Sand Remembers

Desert sand remembers
It was formed by ocean.
100 million years of separation
Does not change its origin
Every tiny grain as unique as our DNA
Traceable to the motion of waves.

Mixed-race baby raised on Ngunnawal Country
Government forced adoption policies
Racist stigma rampant in society
Erased my first mother's heartbeat from memory.

For two decades we chased missing answers
Around and around my cultural heritage
Traced and finally found my birth family.

Reunions textured like desert sunsets
Coloured with joy, relief, anger, grief
Many adoptees never get the chance to meet
Biological families remain a mystery
We become desert sand estranged from the sea.

Recognition of loss, government apologies
Emotional journeys rebuilding identity
Healing begins with remembering.
Desert sand remembers
It was formed by ocean.

Trauma Stories

Our trauma stories
Visit like grieving friends
In need of comforting.

They sit invisibly beside us
Revealing vulnerability
Wanting us to hear them
As they reminisce and weep.

Listen to the truth they speak
Healing is a private conversation
Between the memories we hold
And the trauma stories we release.

Exit Wounds

Double-barrelled heart words
Enclose around our exit wounds

Pain. Shock
Disbelief. Anger
Grief. Hopelessness
Sadness. Numbness

Loss. Loneliness
Solitude. Compassion
Gratitude. Hope
Trust. Love

Bullet holes heal with self-compassion
Transforming hearts from pain through love.

Haunted

Haunted house of broken vows
Poltergeists who will not
Disappear into the call of light
Dreams hidden in these dusty corners
Empty shelves refusing to be filled
Moving boxes wait unopened
Stalled lives are frozen collateral
Phantoms of forgotten love.

Life Hacks

How to relocate your life
How to awaken from numbness
How to unbind from fear
How to create freedom
How to forgive yourself
How to trust yourself
How to love yourself
How to tune into yourself
How to communicate your wishes
How to welcome new friends
How to remember love.

Wondering

What if we
Are the same
Slightly different
Version of the people
We attract?

What if we
Are all the things
That we reject
Because we are
Unconsciously
Rejecting
Ourselves?

What if we
Keep meeting our
Mirrors over
And over again
Each time learning
Something new
about ourselves?

What if we
Read something
That heals part
Of our story that
We never knew
Was broken?

First Impressions

Our young men's faces
Displaced in these places
That raise them.
Outside is erased
They are encased
In the basement of life.

Incarceration replaces
Real chances to thrive.
Survival is a race
While serving their time.
Black Lives Matter
Locked up inside
This price is too high
We are all paying for crime.

The children who miss them
Grow up never knowing
The sounds of the tones
In their own father's voices.
We blame it on bad choices.
Educational disadvantage
Is rarely reported as one
Of the major causes.

Poverty versus Capitalism
Revolving door of recidivism.
If you can buy the best
Legal representation
You might get by
With less discrimination
Serve a shorter sentence.

These are my first impressions.
Junee Correctional Centre
On Wiradjuri Land.
Witnessing my black brothers
Writing poems of loss and hope
And dreaming inside
Their true colours of home.

Ekphrasis Inferno

Inspired by the art of Tanja Ponsford

I don't want to write about this painting
This harrowing red and black rising
Pigment clawing and writhing
Too close to the memories, the colours
Of our Yuin sky on New Year's Eve
Scarlet smoke invoked a decaying midnight
Throughout the first days of this decade.

I don't want to write about this painting
It's the same blood-red moon that stole
40 hours of sunlight bleeding uneasy darkness
Onto our Far South Coast horizon
Leaving only matchsticks of trees behind.
No one knew how long it would be before
We would see our sun shine yellow again.

I don't want to write about this painting
And think about the week my young children
Spent inside, peering out the bedroom window
Into the unsettling smoky nothingness of our yard
Wondering what the fires were consuming
On dairy farms and in small townships around us.

I don't want to write about this painting
And acknowledge its power to move me
Through feelings of helpless grief and loss
This artwork is a sombre reflection
Of the traumatic inferno birth of 2020
Every colour alive with remembrance
Honouring what happened here.

I did not want to write about this painting
But I am grateful to the artist
For creating, sharing and gifting it
The deeper that I look into her painting
The more I can appreciate our bushfire
Stories of courage, strength and survival.

Last Harvest

I left it all on Brown Mountain today
My last harvest before winter
An offering of peace from drama.

I spoke it for the final time
Into the curved sides of the road
Just below each dented safety rail
Released at every hairpin turn
And underneath red cones which warn,
'Do not stop here!'

I have supplanted my last harvest
Words which no longer hold power over me
Plucked like cotton from my soul's unawareness
Misplaced compassion or naivety
Experiences which never brought me joy
Yet I collected them, 200 bales a day
Carried them heavy on my shoulders
Because I refused to tell myself the truth.

As I left it all on Brown Mountain today
I wondered about the Aboriginal name
For this healing dreamscape
Between Yuin and Ngarigo plains.
How did the 'tangata whenua'
the original people of the land
Make use of this transitional place?

A resting ground perhaps
For ocean seekers and spirits alike
Sweeping views from the lookout
Which whisper about centuries
Of intuitive ancient harvest toil
Communities taming mountain ranges
A cultivation space of sages
Travelled everyday unbeknownst
By locals and strangers.

I left it all on Brown Mountain today
My last harvest before winter
An offering of peace from drama.

Remembrance

Alan Maurice Robert Jones 1937–2019

Time is indifferent to grief
One week, two weeks, it's been eight weeks, Dad
Since we last saw you, had our final farewell
Feels like a lifetime of cheerless weeks without you
Time itself hasn't bothered to send us a sympathy card
Time lent you to us for 52 years and 4 months
From the autumn day that you married Mum
And decided to become a family.

It's easy to be angry at Time
When we are happy, Time is too short
When we are troubled, Time never seems to end
We've talked about that phenomenon before.

It's been ten weeks, Dad
Since we sat around your dinner table
Celebrating your 49th Father's Day
With Mum's delicious vanilla cake
Grandchildren piling special offerings
Into your shaky hands as you smiled back
Wondering what all this fuss was about
Homemade cards, chocolates and hugs
A blue and white striped gift bag
Full of books carefully selected by Mum
She would plan ahead for months
Looking for literary treasures you did not
Already have in your impressive collection.

These lovingly wrapped stories
Turned out to be the last paperbacks
You would shine your imagination into
Through glasses that you never liked to take off.
48 hours after your presents were opened
Mum shared them with you in hospital
Too unwell to read them yourself.

When you decided it was almost Time
To release your sore and uncooperative body
Mum knowingly took those books back home
We gathered close reading to you instead
Loving messages from family and friends.

We have given ourselves Time, Dad.
Just as you often advised us
'Don't rush in to anything'
We've reclaimed these past eight weeks
Before gathering in celebration of your life
To reflect on our gratitude for you.

You taught us how to read and think critically about the world
How to reflect on our actions and consider consequences
How to value life, enjoy fun, swim, surf and sail
How to drive cautiously as if 'all the other motorists are idiots'
How to 'Just ignore that behaviour' when being provoked
How to speak our truth and listen to each other
How to be loving and supportive as a family
And the importance of being lifelong friends
Regardless of our differences.

As adults, Dad, you were still there for us
At the other end of the phone or a long drive to visit
In a hundred letters of sage advice
Articles you had written and newspaper clippings
Generous practical wisdom and compassionate understanding
You continued to teach us important life lessons, like:
How to recover from disappointment
How to courageously face challenges
How to be present and patient with ourselves
How to live according to our own values.

As a grandfather you showed our children
How to appreciate old movies
How to keep on with drawing and never give up
How to pull funny faces across the table without anyone else seeing
How to laugh out loud at your silly jokes
How it feels to have a wonderful Poppy who listens and cares.
You passed down your delight in stories
Through music, film, art and literature
Encouraging creativity in two generations.

While Time feels indifferent to grief
Love is indifferent to Time.

Thank you for loving and raising us, Dad.

Heart Solace

Kia Kaha Stay Strong

Where do you go to stay strong?

I go to poetry
Open-minded, open mic poetry
To keep myself connected
With honest words that often
Find themselves neglected
Rejected as too personal
To truly be respected
But we don't give a damn!
We poetry slam
Our subjective perspectives
A bond of truth is our only objective
It keeps us strong!
On this microphone
We want to be safe
To bring everything we own
Kia kaha – we are staying strong

I go to therapy
I drag myself to therapy, regularly
To keep myself accountable
Life can be complex and beautiful
But can be full of strangers
Hard to tell who's dangerous
Have to rearrange this
Thinking I can change these people
Ticking every single box
On my red flag checklist
I work with a therapist
Helps me to measure just
How far I've come
On this journey!
It keeps me strong
Kia kaha – I am staying strong

I go to the sea
Like my ancestors did
I immerse myself
In the Pacific Ocean
To keep myself from drowning
Water holds me up
Weightless
Just enough
To press refresh
On all this pressure
Life is precious
Life WILL get better
Even when stress makes it hard
To see what blesses us
Each time that we lose touch
With who we really are
Kia kaha – stay strong!

I go to drumming
Like my ancestors did
West African djembe drumming
To keep myself grounded
Inside the sacred circles
Rhythms are found in
Heartbeat drum
Unclouds the frowns
Everyone is equal
as the jam goes down
It keeps us strong!
Tuned into harmonic flow
Passionate percussionists know
The freedom of following
Universal pulse
It keeps us strong!
Kia kaha – we are staying strong

Where do you go to stay strong?
Kia kaha – stay strong.

Finally Fine

If I am reading toxic friend
Advice online at 4 a.m.
It's not fine

If I meet with disappointment
Every time I meet you
It's not fine

If I am always the first
To make contact
It's not fine

If you only call me
When you want something
It's not fine

If I feel drained and judged
By how you treat me
It's not fine

If I don't feel joy
When I think of you
It's not fine

If I feel more relaxed
Without you in my life
It's fine

If I am done
With this friendship
It's fine.

Settle

Been away too long on a journey
Now my time is done I'm returning
Making my way home
On these country roads

Following the flow
Of all I think, feel and know
I simply breathe in peace
Breathe out love
And settle.

I am responsible
For the happiness I choose
Unbinding from toxic chemicals
That kept my heart from finding miracles
In the form of kindness sent to heal
And guide me home.

Following the flow
Of all I think, feel and know
I simply breathe in peace
Breathe out love
And settle.

Each present moment distinct
Open arms to welcome life in
Sense the joy in everything
Gratitude is where I begin
Creating the foundation of home.

Following the flow
Of all I think, feel and know
I simply breathe in peace
Breathe out love
And settle.

Release

Release
Go deep
Go deeper
Feel FREE
Feel LOVE

DROP into love
DROP into your body
DROP into this moment
DROP into your body
DROP into love

Feel LOVE
Feel FREE
Go deeper
Go deep
Release

Here Now

Out of nowhere
We are now here
We are here now
Let's be here now

From nothing
There is no thing
That we can't bring
To the present

We are pre-sent
As we descend
On this journey
From there to here

Nowhere to here
We are now here
We are here now
Let's be here now.

Joy Philosophy

Inspired by the art of Amalina Wallace (*Word Spells* – cover art of this poetry collection)

I seek truth
I value vulnerability
It gives me hope
That honesty is still a thing
All I need is the rarity of friends
Surrounding me
Like clarity to begin
A new decade
Completely unafraid
To feel the joy
In the choices that I make.

I seek peace
I let go and release
A convoy of thoughts
Blocking my flow
All I need is to enjoy life
In this present mode
Mindfully.
Forgiveness is a small
Quiet voice expecting me
To listen and agree
Grant myself amnesty
Live by my philosophies
Completely unafraid
To feel the joy
In the choices that I make.

I seek love
To keep me grounded
In this place
I've had enough
of trying to escape
I still believe
Love will find us anyway
We cannot hide
Our light gives us away
We're all here to love
Completely unafraid
To feel the joy
In the choices that we make.

Gabrielle Journey Jones is a poet, percussionist and community builder living on Yuin Country, far south coast, NSW. She has established ongoing projects including Creative Womyn Down Under (2006), Poetic Percussion (2018) and Writing Open Mic Bega 'WOMB' (2021). Gabrielle has shared her spoken word performances as feature poet at local, national and international events for over twenty years.

www.ingramcontent.com/pod-product-compliance
Lightning Source LLC
Chambersburg PA
CBHW062148100526
44589CB00014B/1732